Published by
Mad Swirl Press
Dallas, TX
www.MadSwirl.com

Layout & Design by Johnny Olson
Editing by MH Clay

ISBN: 979-8-9946181-1-0

For Mom & Dad

I have known Chris Zimmerly as a poet and spoken word performer here in the Dallas Area for over 20 years. In my capacity as editor, I have reviewed and interacted with his poetry for almost 16 years.

Chris is one of sharpest thinkers I have known. He is quick witted and creative, as I have witnessed during his spoken word improvisations with other poets – his response is always colored with what the other has spoken (in the improv spirit of "Yes, and…"), yet layers in something else to carry the poem into new places. Part of his process entails thoughtful "push back" on ideas which may not initially "hold water" in his mind; to carry the metaphor a little further, he'll scrutinize the bucket, as well as the contents.

Chris Zimmerly's poetry is magic when his words evoke feelings and images for the reader. Sometimes he makes a verbal abstract collage; each block a pretty picture (word combinations to tickle the ear), but when the reader draws back, a larger picture is revealed, a message embedded (read "NOTE BROKE BLUE").

Sometimes, Chris's work is like an impressionist portrait; few words, partial images, packed with possible story for the reader to imagine. These are a joy to read between his lines. (Read "At Thanksgiving Celebration" and "Obstreperous.")

He can be candid and vulnerable, exposing personal weaknesses and desires, without being confessional, embarrassing the reader with TMI. His plight is everyone's, he offers comfort in camaraderie. Chris is an artful, verbal veteran of the lived-full world (read "Strayling" and "King of Misfit Toys").

He brings a sense of his lived-in space into his work; having grown up in the great American Southwest, deserts, mountains, and stark beauty are imprinted in his poetry. Along with the imagery, he imparts pioneer hope, determination to overcome a ruthless (emotional) environment (read "New Mexico").

His work speaks to the human condition in his unique way. His "unique" is engaging and provocative, a worthy addition to any poetry collection, or collection of poets.

Enjoy your journey through Mirador. Happy reading!

MH Clay
Poetry Editor, Mad Swirl

Mad Swirl

Hootenanny NOW

Song Bag

Mad Swirl

Note Broke Blue

Dad said, "Don't rush the bait,"
A mouthful of hooks
Is all you get.
Fueling the darkness
I abruptly turn
Turn the horseshoes
Backwards
So mice don't
Gnaw my bones.
Invested in wind smoke
Of chimneys
Elusive as the arroyo's
Shaping current
Like tides turning
Against each other
Passing the mad eddy
Swirl, the tug of turnstile
If you smile a smile
In NYC, a thousand
Smiles
End the day.
Each smile a gamble
Wiser from the scars
You know being cut
By the cards.
The longer we live,
The more we know
The dead
Can't help gather up
A bouquet of broken
Wings
Eventually lay
In whatever grave.
The price of love
Wilderness
Blue not so black

On a road like driving up
The Empire State Building.
The road presents faces
Saltwater taffy
Progression
Stretching on
Machine arms
I knew it was summer
The way
The memory comes on me
Car door passing,
Plane in the air
A chandelier with
One candle on fire
The dirt nap is long
And the sleep is slow
When suicide pay ton
Is shifting load to fast
Gravity drift, I see her
As a prairie bird displaying
On the wave of wind.
I drove a big red truck
On a road like driving up
The Empire State Building.
Ok, love is the answer
Passing through tunnels
Love is the question too
I fall through poems
Barely write them
Done as the dance of the
Dancing Albuquerque Lady.
All the men craning their
Necks or nodding yes!
Way out west
Drown in the sunset sun

Through ears
Full of water I hear
Night whisper she comes
Can't get a hold
On the wild sea
Impossible catch
Sunset sun
Here comes the time
To be quick or dead
Because the midnight
Here she comes
Simple gear turn
Click of the clock
The night must
Usher the day
Midnight's promise
Confusion's ghost
Angel or devil
Who holds the sway
The devil fingers
The cold key
Not yet the flesh
Lock will turn
So violence taunts
All dream
All the paper scrap
Will burn
Angel grip on wild sea
Impossible we are
Sunset sun
Midnight burns everyone
I see a face in your face
I am another one of you
I see a face in your face
We are forever
Coming true
Testing all notions
Startles the heart

There is no lock
To this cage
Broke wing
Crossroad generation
Wishing a brave
Clown to rage
I see a face in your face
I am another one of you
I see a face in your face
We are forever
Coming true
Reincarnation
Of the wild sea
Living light sunset sun
Scrapbook memory
Quick and the dead
Midnight bows and is gone
The stars splash
Over my head
Stars splash
Off my shoulder
The last time you press
Your lips on me
The kiss of the
Quick and the dead
There is only one answer
You're hoping to find
I can't give you the
Pleasure you're not mine
Trapped in this season
Caught on the line
Covered in heartbeats
Blood butterflies
Our love a rough stone
Strange cuts late at night
Nothing polished

Nearly light
When voices are
Quieter than thoughts
Star dreams
Scattered form the start
Questions of respect
Question the heart
Why do we come
Together, why do we part?
Running across this
Burning bridge
Ghost in the room
Silent watching
The way night
And daytime part
O the city waits
In the window
You've been
Breaking mirrors
Not in a hurry for dawn
Playing ol' solitaire
Even if you lose this time
One of these days
You will win
Because the losers
Are the winners
Because they let
The winners win
Waiting neither
Here nor there
Hoping against
The disappear
Can't do right
Can't do wrong
Can't feel the night
Can't make the dawn
Things in the heart
Ain't that nice

Feels like skating thin ice
The city waits
In the window
For you to open your eyes
You just keep
Shuffling your deck
Practicing your disguise
Refusing all suggestions
And offers
What are you
So afraid to be
Seems all along you've
Been staring
Into broken mirrors
Come down and see the
Halo smile on the face
What are you doing there
Tearing up
Your heart of ace
Mind racing thinking
Drinking up anger and
Love
Now melancholy
Run with harp
The rain giving up
A blue day sky

July 4, 2008

< untitled >

in each falling leaf
the wind is a little bird
a golden tracer

January 30, 2011

At Thanksgiving Celebration

(she reads in the other room)

She is a Leyden jar
Condensing the currents
Of a properly held
History book.
Lady Leyden Jar is so upset you can't see it.
The fey maenad sits proper and still.
Can you spy? The shadow is
Whipping her wild,
Waking her up in a
Shoebox diorama.

February 8, 2013

Haiku for Eric

Tiny storm diamond
Angel leaps in the lightning
Permanently Yes!

April 27, 2013

Vietnam #4

(for Tim Page)

There are long lines of sweaty men in olive drab
Moving through a low land forest
Hear the heartbeats, the minds drift away
Angry at girlfriends wiggling on some other boy's lap
Thirsty for beers opened with church keys
Hungry for Grandmother's favorite recipe
Sitting in memory's kitchen eating
Slow light, bite by bite.
They are coming past me now
Detonation wires, helmets, holy boots
The click of wedding rings on M-16 stock
The bandages stark white
Now blood red like smoke grenades
Waving into the moment as the radio calls
The static of the radio, incoming rounds
The slogging in leech water
To come to this pulling of the trigger
The burnt gun powder refuse, flames
The song of the shell casings landing in a pile of little bells
The heart is out of control, the eyes are everywhere
The breath a blacksmith's bellows
The movements of this chaos, the battlefield of man
Killing man killing man killing man
The long distance display of the portrait
  Of the faces behind gun barrels
Lit up with fires, Michael Herr says,
  "Vietnam is what we had instead of happy childhoods."

The mechanics of the clouds, the brown rivers,
  The land plowed by bombs
Coughing M-79 grenade launchers burp and burn the woods
They lob explosives into your life
Where brothers in arms carry you, feet dragging

Sips of water, blood wet bandages over your eyes
Over legs torn, mangled bits of a self
Faces point with fingers up the Glory Hill
Daggers of smoke
The soft sharp thud, a brutal helicopter
Auto-rotating in from the clouds
Some of these bodies
Will leave skeletons where they fall.
It is a rock'n'roll flash on a pole as women
   In pink dresses flash peace signs
And part their legs, soldiers dream of pussy
   Waving before their eyes
The cooing choir of soft voices, what the women allow
Arms in the air, drunk for a moment with a cigarette
Nicotine stains gooey on the fingers,
  Breathy fumes of hard alcohol and weed
Flip flops help dry the jungle rot,
Standing on a thousand crates of ammunition
Look down the street
In the air
The roar of the crash
And the suffering
The little yellow mother cradling emaciated crying
Children dusting the bodies with lime
Nuns wailing beyond praying

November 16, 2013

We Have Put Away Our Wings To Stand This Close Together

In the center of a large room is a table.

On the table is a coin.

Everyone knows what the coin says.
"Father, Son, Holy Ghost."

Everyone around here knows that, they go, "Yeah. True."

Around this table there are old men,
Around them Pontificia Cohors Helvetica.
Anyone who tries to get close,
"No Sir. No! No! Ma'am you need to step back."

Believe me. We all know it says, "Father, Son, Holy Ghost."

I know there is
Another side to the coin.

I speak up in the room,
"Ready or not we are evolving…
There once was no Blockbuster Video
Then there was Blockbuster Video
Now there is no Blockbuster Video
Times change."

While you were pondering this
I snatched up the coin from the table.
You know what it says on the other side?

"Mother, Daughter, Spirit of Life."

Oh look, the edge of the coin says something too…
"Understanding, Justice, Peace, Love, Understanding, Justice, Peace, Love"

Are we not looking for all these things?
There are two sides to every coin.

They are coming for me now,
I flip the coin into the air and a voice sings out,

"Mother
Father
Daughter
Son
Spirit of Life
Holy Ghost"

March 14, 2015

Strayling

For many sunsets I went out
Into the fields of my home's
Longitude and latitude,
Desiderium heavy on my heart
Wondering why the winds encourage
Wings casting shadows brushing lips
And then blow them on their way
The gentle fingertips speaking in Braille language
I do not know
My maps are tuned upside down
Which way to go?
Strayling when They showed me the suicide room
I refused to pull the trigger
So, I fell out of the window, window
The breeze was delicious
There I was wing walking on a bi-plane
Buzzing the State Fair of Texas, 1936
The sky a blue bonnet meadow
The wind and I making out
She kissing back my scarf
Like I was, Fancy
She touches with her tongue
Vibrating carillon of thoughts
Tuning atoms to Yes
Witness the altitude
From the edge of a silver wing
Velocity angling me away
I was a fish made of butter in a hot hand
A smile memory melts me
Smearing the seams
Shaking out the stuffing animal
The buttons were unbuttoning
The zippers were unzipping
Shoe laces were untying

A eulogy burdened by desiderium
All was strayling in the wake
I was a comet hat scarecrow
Losing bit by bit the splattering birds
Were taking away my straw
To weave their nidified nests
I was becoming less and less of a real thing
Until I was just fluttering fabric
A flag eaten by the wind
My hat caught in the briar

What.

What?

What
Have I become?

December 19, 2015

No Luche Contra El Corriente

From out of the water, resting in the woods
There you found me like you knew you would.
Liberty, the stroke of midnight's mouth,
In a staring contest with a mirror,
I wonder which one is me.
Now deep enough in the water
The riptide pulls me free,
I am the angel and the echo
Foolishly fighting what must be

March 14, 2015

Black Crow

½ way to Death
Exercising this degrading echo
Snatching up in a beak click
Sharded broken mirror
To offer my Love
A trinket of
Adoration

November 2, 2016

King of Misfit Toys

I bow before you the king of misfit toys
Always wearing a hole
Always leaving a stain
I didn't mean to frighten you
I was just thinking like I do
All these years of darkness fondling the dream
Angel versus devil they seem the same thing
All the colors of hurt wing
When love is the hardest thing
Try to fly on a broken wing
When love is the hardest thing

November 2, 2016

Texas in the Summer

It's so hot
The sweaty business is
We are going
To love or die
Kissing tongue of the sun
Licks the steamy grass
Melting into brown sugar
Yellow sky
Full eyes squinting
Sugar sand squeaks
Wiggling under bare feet
Sleeping in the shade
With a breeze blanket
Covering me today
In poetry dreams
Joy in the waking of words
Breathing deep
Blowing air, 15 dolphins
Leave little plumes
Passing flowers exploding
Like the 4th of July
Lovely

August 5, 2017

New Mexico

I am old crow
Scalpel beak a sonorous horn
My star spangled smile
Seems smooth
On the atomic level
I am jagged as the crest
As the sun comes over the mountain
I stand astride the continental divide
Tears flowing from one eye going to the Pacific Ocean
Tears flowing from the other going to the Atlantic Ocean
Here I stand on this obsidian razor blade
This edge moment time
The dawn line comes
Cartwheels across me now
I remember her because I see
The dawn line reveals
The murder of morning crows
Jettisoned from shadow's rest
Two pairs swing on their wings
So black they flash nitrous
Each swoop in the warming air
Binds their lifetime bond tighter
I am lone crow
She's gone
I clutch my talons tightest on this empty telephone wire quivering
On the edge of I-10 staring west
As the moon is torn from its own face
Leaving black flashing silver
Her smile sparkles
Opalina eyes
They tear like crude rainbows
On the wet stone sharpening our knives
Holding our breath
Kiss kiss kiss

Breath is black hole melancholia
I am lone crow witness
Talons clutched tightest on empty wire
Her shadow wing is passing
Is a kiss on the cheek
5 senses cooking up
Face fireworking 4th of July
Alcoholic hole for eyes
Grab me inside, Melancholia
Just where she wants me
On the heartstring plucking it with her talon
We fly in mad memory
Punctilious Blue Angels
Unaware we uncaring of the dangers of love
Flyingsoclose
That if we touch
We'd fall from the sky and die
So closer and closer we move on the air
I just want
Her talon tap on the heart string
Our shadows hover inside each other
We kiss our beaks
Against the dawn line
Revealing a murder
The jettisoned pairs
Beating their wings
Straddling the continental divide
I am seemingly smooth
But jagged as a mountain mourning.

August 5, 2017

Mad Wet Elves

The unhappiness of sleep paralysis thoughts,
Straitjacket of seaweed and jellyfish tentacles,
A sea hag, heavy as an anchor, rusting on insomniac breath.
Stronger than sleeping pills, trying all the sweat wet pillows again,
What lie will we tell the children
When Santa's Workshop falls through the thin ice at the North Pole?

Will History label us Stupid or Mean?

What lie will we tell the children
When Santa's Workshop comes to rest on the Arctic seafloor?

Santa Claus entombed. Mrs. Claus in Tucson sobbing.
His mad wet elves coming ashore
On the backs of the last polar bears.

The Mont Blanc glacier in reverse has no brakes.
The hotel bar is now on the rocks.
The fighting Poets shout at each other with broken noses,
Blacked eyes, bloodied knuckles, spitting loose teeth at each other
"Stupid!"
"Mean!"

December 22, 2017

Flamingo

Hooker spit in my Listerine,
Magic fingers of the professional
We found each other on Bourbon Street,
Got together for a little party
In a rented room around the corner from the old selling block.
The ghosts blinded Satan
Tabasco sauce pooled in eye sockets.
Jesus drunk with Buddha in the alley
Behind the bar smoking a spliff.
God is with his harem.
Oh friends, Feast!
Eating chilled Jim Morrison brain
As an appetizer.
It's just all a flamingo lobotomy.
Just a flamingo lobotomy.
Flamingo.

December 15, 2018

Oh, Not Again

She has a halo you can
Always almost see
Her kiss will not set
You free
It lingers like a hook
Now you wriggle on
The line
Tasted
You are rotten fruit
On the vine
Wasted
The problem
Wasn't your
Bad advice
It was
That I took
It.

December 15, 2018

Obstreperous

The sky is angry mouth
  where a plum used to be
Quick color the departure walls
O! Lord, I can't believe the news
Everywhere shimmering sudden light

Hey! Do you want to go
  the Featherwood Hospital?
Anodyne stat!
Hey Doctor! Nothing touches
  the tired spot.

Clip the clouds from the fingers
Everywhere simmering sudden light.

Let's check into the Featherwood Hospital.
A tin man, do I have a heart?
Oh no! check my pulse
Quick call a nurse
I'm getting worse!

Wood or feather?
Doctor! Doctor!
What do you prescribe?

May 1, 2019

Illustration by Deon Staffelbach

American Disarray #54

On the two legs
Of a lightning struck sea
An odd dancing scarecrow
Taps out a Morse Code mayday
Poet musing on
An empty glass
The liquor running its legs
Watching her legs
In the last light of the barroom
A witch finger vine stretching
Binding in memory
A bee's map of the world
The monarch proboscis
The ruby-throated hummingbird tongue
Lapping her bell held nectar
The clear tone ringing in the wing beat
Hearing her heartbeat
Earring machinery clanking
Her breathing rhythmic
Faster now,
The stamen brushing
New colors on her dawn

October 5, 2019

Don't Imitate Hemingway

One red husk shell, the smooth barrel gagging

Newly dead Ernie throws his scrambled brains
Quick into the sky as hummingbird turns
Red the predominate color, the second in command
Is green, sick green looney bin locked rooms
Long hallways with echoes
The window's grasping fluctuations
Touchy inside seconds of electroshock therapy
For a minute, only banshee shoulders for the lightning struck

One shell releasing
The last waterfall of thoughts
Swimming in shark jaw water
The warm motion of the falling pieces
Diving to the knees

Nostrils flatulent with snotty brain bubbles
Pupils staggered in terrorizing mirrors
As the soul looks at the body bag
"I love you."
In the last molecule exchange
In the last biting fire

October 5, 2019

Blue Nun

by MH and Zim after being in Deep Ellum

I feel the blue nun, she's on the edge
   of a ready to harvest field of bounty.
The sting and sizzle
Of sister's swizzle
Ignites the inner eruption
Blink. The fields are ablaze, angels screaming
RUN. (You are the one we love, take my hand)
Run. The stumbling nun
Hands on ears
Eyes agog on approaching ever
In the middle of infinity, we exist now.
A roiling rampaging bull knocking down a shotgun shack
Butting us forward
To fall flat or bounce
Ripping open Heaven, be here now
With our snorkels, parachutes, and helmets
Deep dive, girls and boys
Into it, into it now
Dig a little deeper, dig deeper now
Angel or Nothing

December 28, 2019

Regardless of Consequence

The old poet's writing hand lay
Curled like dead songbird feet
On the August sidewalk
The boy pushes on the songbird's chest
One last song snippet
Then quiet bagpipe
The tune forgotten, the blue period of late
Went blackout, new moon allegedly so low
A torn-up paper drawing of a cake
I'll have a slice she said
Pursuing happiness as fast as we can
Each step approaching death
Pursuing happiness as fast as we can
One breath, one heartbeat from rising angel
Pursuing happiness as fast as we can
Tend your fire! You are the signal now
Pursuing happiness as fast as we can
One breath away, one heartbeat away
Another leaf in the street
A phone call unanswered
Oh, you are such an Angel
Here is your participation trophy

April 1, 2020

Milton was murdered.

Lately it seems
All is lost, all is found
All at the same time
If healing is necessary
Ask the Traiteur for help
No payment needed
Milton wishes to hold her closer
"She is light on water to me," he says.

April 17, 2021

For a Stone rolling...

Rilling a mourning bird morning
The Great Charlie Watts
No longer casts a shadow
Our telescopes trained
On his flight into the Light
Our feet got to move

August 29, 2021

Smells Like Old Guitar Strings

Make a funny face cuz you want to
Why is she hiding in shadow
Make a funny face cuz you can
Leaping from silence
The powers refuse to tell the Truth
All the faces in the mirror's memory stare like mullet
Their intention is to divide us
Even from 10,000 light-years away
Your broken-hearted smile
Is a railroad bed
Full of train horn
Blasting at the starlight crossing
Eyes are hung up, gnawing
On shadow and light
You are the Angel
Talking inside into Existing
Littoral zone singing Emily Dickinson's edge of infinity
Then Death is right up in my face
Licking clay from my spirit
Until a ringing bell of light
Is all I am

December 2, 2022

Good Luck

BestGo! BestGo!
Then we are quiet
The moon is down
Clouds marching in
Covering over Orion
Mockingbird sings a little
From the bottlebrush
Oh to read the land and know how
Magnetic perceptors, ley line aware
Star map mind
The migrating passerines
Hurrying laminar flow
Angel, did you wake up you?
On the shelf by the door
Did you find that bottle of red?
Tag! You're It!
All the birth under the waning crescent
After the midnight rain footsteps
A New York toothpick
I believe you believe that
Longing for one's lover
Unexpected trajectories suddenly
A fistball of butterflies opens a light beam
The afternoon heat sounds like summer still
Gone away again into Billie Holiday records
Then just
One
Note
The wind in the leaves
Sounds like deluge
Or chicken thighs on a hot skillet
Our bodies are kites
Flown by angels
We are the root down
Anchoring the bloom
The wind is God laughing
Keeping all the lines tight

March 16, 2024

Ferns

Grow in the grout
Feast on brick
Walking the old streets
One can still smell
Fresh manure in long ago garden plots
Like an olfactory ghost
British and Spanish cannons echo
In the thundery sky
In the wet wind
Praying for better weather
The tide at the turn
Welcoming a bright shiny morning
The feast in the flats
For me, the deep exultation
Within an iced peach

May 30, 2025

Hootenanny NOW

Dirty Zambi Ball Invocation

On the Day of All Souls there is a thinning
  of the veil between Heaven and Earth
All those we've known who have gone on
Our grandparents, our parents, our friends
All spirits on the road of Milky Way highway
Right now they land on the roof like birds
Songbirds in a simple moment singing
As we think about our family and friends flying
Through the lives we know
Passing through us singing songbirds
The fluttering of wings
Setting shots of tequila and tamales on their graves
In our mind the feast
We are now ready to celebrate
We understand that souls are us
Souls are them
Jubilee of song
Dusk birds cresting eternal
Substance of day (dance!)

Balloon

The day after Mom died
Those of us left behind
Sitting outside the nursing home
When a white balloon
Came bouncing towards us
We watched it bounce between
Dad's legs and lodge under his wheelchair
I grabbed it, reading the message
"I Love You" hand written in marker
On the other side "Cheers Bitches"
With crossed champagne glasses
Printed in gold ink.
I gave it to Dad.
"Well, look at that," I said.
He held it with both hands
Saying as best as he could, "I LOVE YOU."
"I LOVE YOU."
"I LOVE YOU."

Pablo Mockingbird

Los niños de montaña verde
Es muy triste porque las lluvias es muerte
¿Dónde esta los sueños del cielo?
¿Dónde esta el tomato?
¿Dónde esta el rio de borracho?
Hombre para corazón del Dios,
Hombre para corazón del mis amigos
Nósotros bailamos los sueños de la luna,
Azul playa, la estrellas nueves
¡Preguntas amore!

What I am trying to say...

The children of the green mountain are very sad
Because the rain is dead
Where are the dreams of the sky?
Where is the tomato?
Where is drunk river?
Hungry for the heart of God
Hungry for the heart of my friends
We dance the dreams of the moon
Blue beach, new stars
Questions of love!

Pompeii

I.

  Pushy Italian boot bully
  Vesuvius trips
Vesuvius is void artist in a fit
Dulling wild chisels working up volcanic orgasm
Boiling possibility on the vine
Choking out marketplace haggle
Blind and barefoot,
Nydia fingerprints her mark, listening
Lava laughs
Pyroclastic pummeling Nydia
  Curvy on memory paper
Suddenly the wash of face
Vesuvius drops lava tool

II.

  As with everything spirit
  We come and go
With your hand on my shoulder
Filter vision with hair
Touch your fingers with my fingers
For an hour we hold hands
Hold your heartbeat up to my head
We are backed up

Guam

No songbirds sing on the island of my birth
Immense vibrations accompany napalm
The brown climbing snakes swallow songbird song
Her flesh is charring, she moves like a Chinese firework
No songbirds sing on the island of my birth
The pilot calls, "Feet wet." Crossing out over the ocean
Planes bringing the brown climbing snake from Vietnam
The fire is out on the little girl now, she runs on the road
No songbirds sing on the island of my birth
The pilot is smoking, counting bullet holes in his Crusader fuselage
The brown climbing snakes slither up out of toilets, infiltrating transformers
The little girl screams through the melted halo of her mouth
The pilot forgets how to fly drinking himself in suburbia
No songbirds sing on the island of my birth

A Simple Friday Night in High School

Drunk child mutated with madness
Filled with anger,
Sadness.
Rushing through the city,
A red streak of danger.
Passing out at home,
No sense of safety
Only loss.

This joke is no longer funny
Casual flirtations
With drunk car death
Hungry diseased keening
Cooling corpse
Behind the broken wheel
Useless as unopened condom
Unspoken word of truth

Sip of Vodka

Grozny is full of tracers
Tears icicle in fall
Uncontrollable static cross ripped tympanum
The shutter left open
Collects light
In a frantic moment of incoming
Every molecule skips
All is bright
Decaying blood seeps
From sponge sized bits of a man

Never Get on the Boat

The rats are leaping off the anchor chain
Hurrying rust to the bottom of the harbor

All the sailors carry the corpse face openly
When they smile teeth fail them

The shadows are thin from not eating
The captain is sleeping on his one leg like a flamingo

Death strides up the gang plank
  Tapping electric cane, "Let us depart, time is blue."
On the tide turn, slide into current bending
  When the reef eats the hull, sharks lured
Like Americans to neon crossroads
  The corpse faces are put away like Halloween masks
Shark teeth settle, lost seamen congregate
  The coral choral sings a mermaid song
Somewhere is a dirty cloud, tuna net
  Control algorithm starving humans

Someday soon as a Mexican cigarette, south of the border
A dusty street angel will wake up a girl
The Sea of Cortez gray whale lagoon
Birthed out of a ring of nurse whale's sweet breath
She might stroll streets
Singing to birds disguised by big leaves
For her eardrum signal there is translation
Birdsong into words,
"We are angels, good morning, we are angels, good morning, we are angels, good morning."
There in clean sky and clean clouds
Of clean water falling to clean land

Running into clean rivers emptying into clean ocean
Spyhopping gray whales
Singing humpbacks, echolocation of porpoises
Riding the crest of a wooden sailboat
The spitting masthead throwing mad vapor
The course of wind driven laughter
Light bounding as glint
Wishing for and catching
The light of love

Doctor de Bueno's Plywood Painting

"You're too deep, come out of there. Beach is closed."
- City of Chicago Lifeguard to Doctor de Bueno

Three days after breaking up, Doctor de Bueno stands shin deep
In Lake Michigan, so disturbed he drills a halo in the sky

Angry blue iris blood vessels in a hawk head
Focus over a burnt orange

Twisted tar strangles itself, drips
Turning blue sky into violet pansy, violent green
Then ball point blue
Oh, I miss her retreating hot cave,
Her pink ribbons
    Run out like a pen losing its ink

Radio Wave Haiku

Time to harvest now
Deep Earth cornucopia
Fuel for travelling

Awbeg River

From the Bridge House
Walking downhill
Crows cawing flapping
Shadows within shadows
In the crooked tombstone teeth
Of the church's graveyard
By the Awbeg River
A metal gate unlocked
Worry heavy as a backpack of rocks
Her panic in the hospital
Twisting the trail
Across floodplain meadow
Full of bees busy
Inside Irish flowers, the river
Was murmuring like friends
In the next room
The sun was a friend too
Slowing steps so much
I sat down
Then laid back into the grass and flowers
Soaking up the light
Sky blue cradled by the meadow frame
The river speaks in thoughts
Birds are the sky
Tracers weaving the warp and woof
The fabric waking this moment
This life where I see children
Coming up with the flowers
Buzzing with busy bees flying
In the mouths of a bird
The Awbeg keeps talking
What the Awbeg knows
We come and bring words of Love
And we flow
And the river flows
And grows over
After we are gone

Early Again (Mirthful)

Up early again in the linger
Of night (star splashed)
After all the whip-o-wills
Are done singing,
We wait patiently
On the enchanted world branch
Whitebird singing a tiny feather song
Poet in a sad room
Sweeping up the last lost hair
She left when
She left
The birds and I on one enchanted world branch
Silence holding the tongue
Turning the ear to the creaky
Machinations of our wet blue sphere
Evolving the dream into light
We gamble on the arrival
This new day's dilated cry
Bound in love she shudders
As his wing wind passes
Oddly in two worlds
Blood bones (shouting shadows)
Exclaiming light
Here bodies the instrument (singing)
There beyond the distortion of death's noise
The face inside that rests in always
If the angel melancholic
Can't stem wilderness tears
The whip-o-wills and I frolic
Shattering the last star ushering day
Hoping the Angel will join in
Without offering our hand—how else would we know?
I don't know what else to do.

Song Bag

Jubilee

If I wrote a letter to tomorrow would she answer me
I swear I'll be careful with my wishes I just want the Jubilee
Paint it as a picture everyone smiling you'll see
Passing out invitations to everyone I see
Please won't you come on down to the Jubilee

If I wrote a letter to this day what would I say
Compliments to the weather, the smile you wear that way
Sometimes you and me a theater of madness
Sometimes we're lovely when we do our best
Time to be grateful down at the Jubilee
Please come on down, down to the Jubilee

If I wrote a letter to the past what should I say
Lingers of emotion, don't be stuck in apology
Only time now to celebrate you and me
Sometimes simple success is all we want to be
Please come on down to the Jubilee (Come on!)
Please come on down to the Jubilee (Come on!)

Bear's Mouth

Cool precious water, bear's mouth full of bees and honeycomb
Will we kiss in a room full of wild roses
Or are we diamond scared fools bound to fold our hands
Cool clear water, is the prize worth the price

Thank you thank you thank you so sweet to me
If I were a religious man I'd say
You were an angel sent to me

But I just feel the wind, like the sun on my face
I think rain sings a pretty song
Before I eat, I say, "Grace"

Don't want to kiss you, you're not my bride
Don't want to mistreat you
Or take you for a ride

Just a simple thank you, got a friend who don't pray
Just hope to wake up wishing
Everything will be ok

Cool precious water, bear's mouth full of bees and honeycomb
Will we kiss in a room full of roses
Or are we diamond scared fools bound to fold our hands
Cool precious water, is the prize worth the price

Constant Crossroads

Welcome my Friend
To constant crossroads
Persistence earns the goal
This is the beginning
This is the end
All the pieces of the middle
See the scarecrow peer
In the crow's mouth
There are no diamonds there
Suddenly the rain arrives
Like a fist full of marbles
You must decide
Or stumble in the lightning
To some you seem an angel
To others a devil
It is hard to be the man in between
Some say mine for gold
Dig until your hands are bones
Some say better fall in love

Rabbit's Heart

Last leaf trees of November
See the wind walking the rain
I hear her call out to falling water

We can't see the wind but we think it is there
Caress your smile, choirs in our hair
Waking up the dreamsong on both sides of the mirror

Her pink lipstick invents a cool kiss
Refuse to trap love in a cage
Run rabbit run the heart always free

Red wine sunshine
Blue sky blues
Gathering of cloudlets white
Everywhere with you
Everywhere with you
Everywhere with you
Is wild

As we feel that feeling once again
Lonely as one cloud her quiet shadow
As you hold the rabbit's heart in your hand
As you hold the rabbit's heart in your hand
Hold the rabbit's heart in your hand

Goodbye Champaign

End of the day when the sand turns blue
End of the long hot season with you
Raise our glasses so we can see
Three musketeers here at the table with me

You've been tending the lighthouse
I've been lost at sea
You've been tending the lighthouse
Keeping the light on for me

When we drop everything
Let it all go
All that's left is angel
All those angels we know

Sunset heart so big, beating so fast
Sunset crying on the way home
Yeah, we're kissing goodbye Champaign
Yeah, we're kissing goodbye Champaign

Ain't No Rainstorm That Heals Like You

If you'd only speak to me
Then I would reply
The ghost and I talking
She touches me I ask her why?
We discussing reality late at night
Caught up in the bright light morning
Taking the medicine
Keeps making me sick
Oh Lord, could I sing my way out of this
Crowded darkness
Swinging lantern
Illuminating circle
Family and Friends
Before the beginning
After the end

New New Orleans Blues

We are the moments of dawn
Before the morning comes along
Restless spirits refuse to lay down
We are the moments of dawn
Morning comes along
Here comes the line of light to New Orleans town
Stuttering streetcar on St. Charles Avenue
Heading toward the river, all broke up and blue
Swallow the Christmas lights in the vampire's nest
In your dreams see it, find a solution that is best

We're all in this together
There is nothing else to do
Break your face with smiles
Other dreams still come true
Inside the cathedral
Her drunk broke down tears
She'd rather make any guy
Then answer to the angels round here
Old Hickory gallops around the square
That bullet buried so deep
No surgeon would dare
Dead sleep in boxes, sleep above the ground
Classic lady wishes me around

Encourage this voodoo
Don't hold back be you
Share the secret how we've come to this
The ghost of her hurricane still so naked raw and pain
With no home to even hang a new dress
The levee's mouth is wide open
She trembles her last kiss
Her breast hot against my chest
She trembles in the lonely pain
Kicking at the roof, Mama
Come on let me win
Will it be sunshine
or rain again

Mobile

Drink my spirits from a jar
Smoke on the whiskey we've gone too far
Oh Moon hold close
You are a strange feather
Just like that the stars are gone

Allergic to lightning, thunder gets me high
Jumping out of my second skin flying
The weather is rough, people say I'm tough
I decided to stay here with you
We are always in the heart

Don't you give me that evil eye
I'll grab ahold of a cool, cool comet tail
Outside the inside smiles are contagious
Outside the inside singing the unsung
We are always in the heart

Why does is it rain every time, every time I drive to Mobile?
Why does it rain every time, every time I drive to Mobile?
You're lucky I didn't knock, knock you out in St. Louie.
Why does it rain every time, every time I drive to Mobile?

The Caged Bird Sings

I only lost a dream, the caged bird sings
Refusing to bend on a broken wing she depends
In this new silent spring where no birds sing

The line just hangs there empty the wine whistles alone
Can't seem to kick these habits in the vineyard overgrown
Go away we are lovers talking, please lover please

The cage bird sings
I only lost a dream
The caged bird sings
Only things of dreams
The caged bird sings
Open door of dreams

Queen of the Underworld Spies

All alone with my cane sister
She says I'm a sinister mister
She would be one to be in on the know
She is the Queen of the Underworld Spies
So very hard to meet her
With her ever-changing disguise
Queen of the Underworld Spies

She can tune her own guitar
Deciphers the meaning of dreams
Rains light on every seed assuming the scene
She is Chicago Blues
He is fuss bucket Dallas news
They both know what to do
She is the Queen of the Underworld Spies

You smell like a casino she said
Glazed eyes hot breath
Wandering around like a snake
Looking for the Jackpot (Jackpot!)
She is the Queen of the Underworld Spies
So very hard to meet her
Her ever-changing disguise
She is the Queen of the Underworld Spies

Hey Becky Thatcher

Hey Becky Thatcher
You sure had Tom Sawyer
Who had Huck Finn on the run
Lashed raft push the river, riding on the waters
A run-away slave ain't no sin
Aunt Polly wants her fence whitewashed
Work ain't work when it's a joy
Play with your toy angel
We'll be resting on islands forming in the river
So sorry I forgot
What went wrong animal
What went wrong my friend
It is a fool's parade to fight the deaf, dumb and blind man
None of us is qualified to advise nothing
Though I think we both know the dangers of the black out trap
Let's leap like rabbits in the briar invisible
Let's rest on islands forming in the river
Hey Becky Thatcher
You sure had Tom Sawyer
Who had Huck Finn on the run
Lashed raft push the river, riding on the waters
A run-away slave ain't no sin

Hitchhiker

There is a song
In these notes I play
A story to be told
By the breezes of the day
How it will end
Perhaps someone knows
Lord, they ain't talking
Guess I'll keep on playing
Just to see where it goes

Travel by train
Travel in the air
On the edge of the grand highway
Ask me if I dare
Picked up an old hitchhiker
By the side of the road
Outside of Hatch, New Mexico
He needed a ride
I needed to go

Riding in a pick-up truck
Across New Mexico
Heading into Arizona
To lighten ourselves
From this load
The old sunburnt hitchhiker
Bows his head in prayer
Every time the wheel is turning
We are on the way home

We got to talking
Talked a whole lot
He never said nothing
That I forgot
Strangely familiar
The lilt in his voice
When I let him out in the Old Pueblo
He walked away like a ghost

Must have been a friend of mine
Different space different time
Felt as though I watched a shadow
Shadow of myself
Embracing another lifetime
All I did was wish you well

Well, I wish you well, I wish you well
Well, I wish you well, I wish you well
Well, I wish you well

Cowboy Art - Hico. Tx. '91
PART TO

Chris Zimmerly has been writing poetry for over four decades. After graduating from the University of Arizona, he has been active in the Dallas Poetry Community since 1995. He was busy in Dallas at the turn of the century performing in the Slam and coffee house/ art scenes. *Get in the Mother Lovin' Car,* a collection of poems and short stories was published in 1999 by San Saba Press. He hosted Bohemia Open Mic at the Velvet Hookah in Deep Ellum before becoming a regular at the Mad Swirl Open Mic for the last 20 years. He was a featured poet at the *Blackwater Poetry Festival* in Ireland in 2016. Chris has been published in multiple *Best of Mad Swirl* anthologies, *Mad Swirl VI: Blue Note Issue, Tartan, The Word, Post Amerikan,* on *Slams,* Volume 1: Dallas-March 1999 CD, on multiple occasions performing an opening poem at the Bayou Rendezvous in New Orleans during Jazz Fest and had a haiku read on "Travel with Rick Steves" Radio Show. Check out Mad Swirl's podcast *Inside the Eye!* for a one-on-one interview. Chris has performed poetry in Texas, Louisiana, Florida, Colorado, New Mexico, Arizona, California, Arkansas, Indiana and Illinois. Picking up the guitar three decades ago, Chris combines his lyrics with his own music and with other music partners, playing in bands along the way: Wagon Wheel Illusion, Alchemy Brats, Hootenanny Campfire, Pecan Tree, Ambergris, CZWP and Sasquatch Grandma. More to come soon.

www.ingramcontent.com/pod-product-compliance
Lightning Source LLC
LaVergne TN
LVHW011049110826
845149LV00015B/3423

* 9 7 9 8 9 9 4 6 1 8 1 1 0 *